Koch, Carl

LOVE VIRTUE

DAILY PRAYERS FOR VIRTUE

# Love

by
Carl Koch



Saint Mary's Press
Christian Brothers Publications
Winona, Minnesota

Genuine recycled paper with 10% post-consumer waste.
Printed with soy-based ink.

The publishing team included Carl Koch, series editor; Stephan Nagel, development editor; Jacqueline M. Captain, manuscript editor; Amy Schlumpf Manion, typesetter; Maurine R. Twait, art director; pre-press, printing, and binding by the graphics division of Saint Mary's Press.

The acknowledgments continue on page 92.



Printed in the United States of America

Printing: 9 8 7 6 5 4 3 2 1

Year: 2004 03 02 01 00 99 98 97 96

ISBN 0-88489-383-9

■ ■ ■

*to Joyce—*

At our age the imagination
    across the sorry facts
        lifts us
to make roses
    stand before thorns. . . .

(William Carlos Williams)

# *Contents*

# *Foreword*

> "I was a revolutionary when I was young and all my prayer to God was 'Lord, give me the energy to change the world.'
>
> "As I approached middle age and realized that half my life was gone without my changing a single soul, I changed my prayer to 'Lord, give me the grace to change all those who come in contact with me. Just my family and friends, and I shall be satisfied.'
>
> "Now that I am an old man and my days are numbered, my one prayer is, 'Lord, give me the grace to change myself.' If I had prayed for this right from the start I should not have wasted my life."
>
> (Bayazid)

We have enough evidence that the world needs to change. Each day we witness violence, poverty, hate, and ignorance both close and far. In the face of these realities, we may fall into the same trap as the Sufi mystic Bayazid, directing our attention to all those other people out there who need changing. We may forget the words of Jesus:

> Do not judge, so that you may not be judged. . . .
> Why do you see the speck in your neighbor's eye, but

> do not notice the log in your own eye. . . . Take the log out of your own eye, and then you will see clearly to take the speck out of your neighbor's eye.
>
> (Matthew 7:1–5)

Jesus' meaning is clear: we cannot expect virtue—this inner readiness to do moral good—from our neighbor if we do not expect, nurture, and develop it in ourselves. The reverse is also true: the virtue that we nurture, develop, and reflect in our life calls forth virtue in others.

## *Planting the Seeds of Virtue*

We begin to develop virtue where the Sufi mystic's prayers left off, by turning the care of the world over to God and by taking care of our own soul.

To deal with his tendency toward harshness, Vincent de Paul told a friend: "I turned to God and earnestly begged him to convert this irritable and forbidding trait of mine. I also asked for a kind and amiable spirit." Vincent's movement toward God involved a surrender to God's presence and power. His prayer also manifested Vincent's need for moral conversion. Vincent knew that living like Christ and clothing himself in Christ's virtues had to begin with knowledge of his own sins and blessings. Times of prayer, the honest opening and offering of ourselves to God, provide the context for a change of heart, mind, and will to happen.

Praying for virtue may be roughly compared to tending a garden. "It was a great delight for me," writes Teresa of Ávila, "to consider my soul as a garden and reflect that the Lord was taking a walk in it." Prayer—the celebration of gratefulness for the goodness in life—invites God to walk in our garden. Prayer welcomes the Master Gardener to plant the seed of virtue within us. Prayer prepares the soil for the seed when it opens our fears, doubts, sins, and goodness to the gaze and grace of the Creator.

## *The Three Brilliant Flowers: Faith, Hope, and Love*

In the garden of the soul, the virtues of faith, hope, and love form the centerpiece. Traditionally called theological virtues, they come as free gifts from God and draw us to God. We cannot earn these virtues; God has already freely planted them in our soul.

However, these virtues need tending. In prayer, we can open our heart, mind, and will to God's grace. We embrace and open ourselves to this grace by pondering and dialoging with God about what we believe, how we hope, and the ways we love. When we ponder the Scriptures and examine our beliefs, we nourish faith. When we meditate on the goodness of God's creation, on friendships, and on all of God's gifts to us, we nourish hope. When we pray for loved ones, consider how we love, empathize with those needing love, and celebrate the love given to us, we nourish love.

## *A Harvest of Plenty—the Moral Virtues*

Faith, hope, and love are further nurtured as we develop the moral virtues of courage, justice, prudence, moderation, temperance, forgiveness, and so on. Saint Augustine and other spiritual teachers maintained that the moral virtues are expressions of faith, hope, and especially love. For instance, in the face of danger to a loved one, people find courage that they never dreamed of having. Living prudently—figuring out what is right in a given situation—becomes easier when love reigns in our heart and focuses our will.

Paradoxically, as we develop the moral virtues, we also nourish faith, hope, and love in ourselves. For example, as we grow in justice we begin to look out for the well-being of other people. In short, we grow more loving. Temperance—creating harmony within ourselves—fosters hopefulness.

## *Growing a Destiny*

We change ourselves by changing the small assertions of self, namely our acts, beginning with an act of prayer. The following wise adage—another garden image—provides a helpful way of thinking about this question and about growing in the moral virtues:

Plant an act; reap a habit.
Plant a habit; reap a virtue or vice.
Plant a virtue or vice; reap a character.
Plant a character; reap a destiny.

Developing our character and destiny begins with the acts that we plant each day, whether consciously or unconsciously. We give shape to our life by each action we take, day by day. A regular pattern of actions becomes a habit. Eventually, our habits determine the shape of our character.

Our character is the combination of our virtues and vices. Our destiny is what finally becomes of us, which depends on the character we build in response to God's grace. A Christlike destiny begins forming with every act of moral virtue. When we pray to be just, temperate, or moderate, when we pray for courage, honesty, and a forgiving spirit, we acknowledge our dependence on God's grace, but we also give our attention to the development of these virtues. Meditating on how these virtues are or are not present in our actions nourishes the seeds of these virtues within us. Praying for moral virtue is planting, weeding, and watering virtuous acts. The harvest of such prayer will be plentiful: We change the world by changing the small part of it that we are. An old adage says, "Prayer does not change things. Prayer changes people, and people change things." Prayer brings us to the God of love who wants us to live fully, to love, to believe, and to hope. If we open ourselves to God's grace, we will change. Then we can change things.

## *The God of Weeds*

Developing habits of moral virtue takes conscious, consistent effort. The late Robert Hutchins, former president of the University of Chicago, remarked:

> Habits may be lost, corrupted, or diminished. The violin player who stops playing and the tennis champion who stops practicing will soon fall from their lofty eminence. And though the moral virtues are among the most durable of all goods, they, like other habits, may be lost, and for the same reasons.

Like all gardens, the garden of our soul can become tangled and overgrown with weeds, or parched and withered from lack of water. Virtue, like a garden, fails to thrive without attention and care. Prayer tends the garden. It also allows us to ask for forgiveness so that we can start again when we have left the garden untended. The loving God is always waiting to sustain us and draw us back to full life. Our God is the God of Hosea who says about sinful and ungrateful Israel: "'I led them with cords of human kindness, with bands of love. I was to them like those who lift infants to their cheeks. I bent down to them and fed them'" (11:4).

## Praying for Virtue

In the epistle to the Ephesians, Paul tells the community to put on virtue, God's armor:

> Be strong . . . in the strength of [God's] power. . . . Take up the whole armor of God. . . . Fasten the belt of truth around your waist, and put on the breastplate of righteousness. As shoes for your feet put on whatever will make you ready to proclaim the gospel of peace. With all of these, take the shield of faith. . . .
>
> (6:10–16)

To help us clothe ourselves in the armor of virtue, the prayers in this book follow an ancient pattern: listen *(lectio)*, reflect *(meditatio)*, and respond *(oratio)*. Here are some suggestions for using the prayers:

**Listen.** Each prayer begins with a passage from the word of God, the wisdom of a spiritual writer, or a story. Read the passage attentively at least once, or better yet, several times. Concentrate on one or two sentences that touch your heart; ponder their meaning for you and their effect on you. This type of listening is called *lectio divina,* or "divine studying." The passages are intended to inspire, challenge, or remind you of some essential aspect of the virtue.

**Reflect.** Once you have listened to wisdom, each prayer invites you to reflect on your own experience. This is *meditatio,* or "paying attention." Each reflection can help you attend to how God has been speaking to you in your past and present experience. If you keep a journal, you may want to write your reflections there. Take the reflection questions with you while you go about your day; ponder them while you drive, wait for an appointment, prepare for bed, or find any moment of quiet.

**Respond.** Each reflection ends with a prayer of petition and thanks. In *oratio,* we ask God for the help we need in nurturing the virtue. We should never be shy in asking God for help. After all, Jesus tells us many times to seek God's grace, and he assures us that God's help will come. Indeed, the word *prayer* means "to obtain by entreaty." The petitionary prayer reminds us that we are truly dependent on the goodness and love of God for developing the virtue. The response prayer usually gives thanks for the gifts God has showered upon us already. Giving thanks is another way of waking us up to all the wonders of God's love.

Try reading the prayers aloud. They gain a different feel and power. Or use one line as a prayer throughout the day. Plant the prayer line in your heart as you repeat it while having a cup of coffee, washing your hands, or sitting at your desk.

## *Starting Points*

**Create a sacred space.** Jesus said, "'When you pray, go to your private room, shut yourself in, and so pray to your [God] who is in that secret place, and your [God] who sees all that is done in secret will reward you'" (Matthew 6:6). Solitary prayer is best done in a place where you can have privacy and silence, both of which can be luxuries in the life of a busy person. If privacy and silence are not possible, create a quiet, safe place within yourself, perhaps while riding to and from work, sitting at the dentist's office, or waiting for someone. Do the best you can, knowing that a loving God is present everywhere.

**Move into sacred time.** All of time is suffused with God's presence. So remind yourself that God is present as you begin your prayer. If something keeps intruding during your prayer, spend some time talking with God about it. Be flexible, because God's Spirit blows where it will. Gerald May speaks to this when he says,

> The present . . . contains everything that is needed for lovingly beginning the next moment; it seeks only our own willing, responsive presence, just here, just now. . . . There are no exceptions—not in physical pain, not in psychiatric disorder or emotional agony, not in relational strife. . . . Love is too much with us for there to be any exceptions.

Come to prayer with an open mind, heart, and will. Trust that God hears you and wants to support your desire to nourish virtue in your life. Prayer strengthens our will to act. Through prayer, God can touch our will and empower us to live according to what we know is true.

Prayer nourishes the seeds of virtue that are planted in our soul. Listening to wisdom fertilizes the seed. Reflecting on or attending to the virtue waters the seed. Responding with petitionary and thanksgiving prayers shine light on the seed. After the thirty-one days of prayer about love, you will have planted the seed in rich soil and will likely understand the virtue more fully and have deeper insight into how the virtue plays out in your own life.

God be with you as you pray for the virtue of love and nurture it in your heart, mind, and will. You will be a power for the good of us all.

Carl Koch
Editor

# Introduction

## Love Is the Good Life

Love is the essence of much music, poetry, and literature, and the subject of endless speculation. People fight and die for it. Love of God has inspired people to embrace martyrdom. Without love, lives are empty and tragic.

Love appears in the human condition in so many forms that at first it might seem impossible to speak of love as one reality. The word *love* encompasses the passionate love of a newlywed couple as well as the almost unspoken love of two close friends, acts of charity as well as the prayerful appreciation of God's gifts to us.

Love is the center of meaning in a Christian life, indeed, of full human life. In his classic, *Love and Will,* psychologist Rollo May said, "Life comes from physical survival; but the *good life* comes from what we care about." Love is our ecstasy, and failed love, our agony. Loving is the font of our greatest joy, but when love is frustrated it can also be the source of our profoundest anger, bitterness, and hurt.

The Christian tradition describes love as one of the three theological virtues: that is, a virtue that is a gift from

God and draws us to God (*theos*, in Greek). We can strive to develop the moral virtues like justice and prudence—these help us love more fully. But love itself cannot be acquired; it is pure gift, given by God through others.

Love is lived faith and hope; it is the crown of all the virtues and an intimate participation in God's life; love is embedded in the scriptural view of life:

- Jesus gave this blunt answer when asked which was the most important commandment: "'The first is . . . "you shall love . . . God with all your heart, and with all your soul, and with all your mind, and with all your strength." The second is this, "You shall love your neighbor as yourself." There is no other commandment greater than these'" (Mark 12:29–31).
- Paul's first letter to the Corinthians says, "And now faith, hope, and love abide, these three; and the greatest of these is love" (13:13).
- The first letter of John declares: "God is love. Whoever loves dwells in God, and God in them. Those who claim to love, but hate their sisters and brothers are liars because those who do not love people whom they can see cannot love God whom they have not seen" (1 John 4:16–20).

## What Is Love?

Defining love is almost as impossible as defining God, but we know love when we experience it. We perhaps understand it even better when we feel its absence, when we experience hate, betrayal, distrust, or indifference. In *The Awakened Heart,* Gerald May comments:

> We can categorize love in endless ways, devise countless strategies to make it happen as we wish, yet always it remains beyond our control. We know that love is beyond our control because it keeps hurting us. We would like to experience the joy and energy of love without being vulnerable to its pain, but there is no way to do that. To love is to care, to care is to give ourselves, and giving ourselves means being willing to be hurt.

The grace of love urges us—heart, mind, and will—to nurture and foster the good of others in whatever ways we can. Love invites us to embrace and affirm ourselves. Love always draws us close to God.

Rather than attempting a definition of love, Paul tells the Corinthians what love is and what it is not in terms of the moral virtues:

> Love is patient; love is kind; love is not envious or boastful or arrogant or rude. It does not insist on its own way; it is not irritable or resentful; it does not rejoice in wrongdoing, but rejoices in the truth. It bears all things, believes all things, hopes all things, endures all things.
>
> (1 Corinthians 13:4–7)

Then Paul says, "Pursue love" (14:1). We pursue love in many ways.

**Loving ourselves.** Perhaps the least understood way of pursuing love is loving ourself, but it is essential to loving anyone else: """You shall love your neighbor as yourself""" (Mark 12:31). This commandment implies that we do love ourselves.

Self-love begins with self-acceptance, that is, discovering and valuing our gifts and griefs, our virtues and vices. Self-love fosters our best qualities and forgives our worst. Mostly, self-love comes as we try to see ourselves from God's vantage point, and God loves us unconditionally. Self-love permits us to offer God all that we are.

**Friendship.** Friends mutually and equally care for each other; they are loyal, and supportive of each other and share a common view of the world. Friends are capable of helping each other to achieve what is good. Ted and Iggy are great examples of friendship:

> Ted and Iggy walked into the diner together at exactly 7:00 a.m., just like they had for the last thirteen years since retirement. Every Friday morning they met at church for Mass and then headed to the Chat 'n' Chew Diner for what they both called a "high-cholesterol, one-my-wife-will-never-fix-me" breakfast.
>
> "Hi, Margaret!" they both chimed in.
>
> "Must be Friday at 7:00 if you two are here!" she chided, friendly.
>
> "You bet!"
>
> "Margaret, I believe you get prettier each Friday morning."
>
> Margaret beamed. "You old jokers just sit down. I know what you'll order, so don't even say it." She bustled around, readying their standard.
>
> Ted and Iggy eased into "their" booth. If a stranger had come in and seen them, that person would have thought at one minute that they were planning a bank robbery—their heads bent close together as they talked furiously fast—and at another minute that they didn't know each other—their faces still, in calm repose.

The two men were seventy-eight years old. They had gone to high school together and had grown up in the same neighborhood. Ted had taken a job as a postal worker after high school, and Iggy had sold men's clothing at one of the big stores downtown. Each had been the other's best man and godfather to the other's first child.

During World War II, Iggy had been left behind at home because of a rheumatic heart. Every fifth of July since the war, Iggy would tell his wife that that same day in 1942 had been the worst of his life. He had gone with Ted down to the train that would take him to San Francisco and then to the war with Japan. Iggy had grieved because Ted was going to war without him.

"Agnes," Iggy would tell his wife, "that's one of the few times I ever cried. I never thought I'd see Ted again."

When Ted had returned from the war, Iggy had been there at the station. The two old friends had shaken each other's hand, but becoming overwhelmed with emotion, they had hugged each other joyfully. "I didn't think you would make it without me!" Iggy had yelled happily.

Then, just for a moment, the smile had left Ted's face. He had looked at his friend seriously, "I wasn't so sure that I would make it either."

After Ted's return, they never talked about the war. With only a few short absences from each other, the two men had stayed close, watched their children grow up and move away, argued about sports, consoled each other when they felt hassled, fished together, and called each other regularly to see what was up.

At age seventy, Iggy had "got religion," as Ted said, and he had started going to Mass almost every morning. Now Ted would join him on Fridays, mumbling that once a week was "okay for Jesus, why not for us?" Then the pair would head for their breakfast at the Chat 'n' Chew Diner.

In addition to being loyal and supportive and sharing a similar view of the world, our friends let us pull off our masks and be ourselves. Such deep intimacy is experienced with only a few friends in life, but all friendships are important.

**Erotic love.** Maybe the most celebrated love is erotic, the desire two people have for union of their bodies as well as their souls. What distinguishes erotic love from other expressions is the yearning for sexual expression of that love. This is the love described in many passages from the Song of Solomon.

> Set me as a seal upon your heart,
> as a seal upon your arm;
> for love is strong as death,
> passion fierce as the grave.
> Its flashes are flashes of fire,
> a raging flame.
> Many waters cannot quench love,
> neither can floods drown it.
> If one offered for love
> all the wealth of his house,
> it would be utterly scorned.
>
> (Song of Solomon 8:6–7)

**Charity.** Charity starts with the belief that all people are our spiritual sisters and brothers, children, and parents. So we treat everyone as we would wish ourselves to be treated if we were in their situation. The Christian Scriptures are filled with stories of Jesus healing blind people and lepers, feeding the hungry, and raising the dead. Jesus stated that nurturing love will be the chief criterion for separating the "sheep" from the "goats" at the Last Judgment, when he will speak these words:

"Come, you have been blessed by God with the inheritance prepared for you from the time of creation. For I was hungry, and you fed me. I thirsted, and you provided me with something to drink. . . ."

The righteous will ask Christ: "But when did we do all these acts of charity to you?"

And Jesus will declare: "In truth, when you did these things to any one of the least of your sisters and brothers, you did them to me."

(Matthew 25:34–40)

**Parental love.** Closely related to charity or nurturing love is parental love. Parental love includes the affirmation of, care of, and responsibility for one's children. Parents exercise their power for the good of children who cannot feed, clothe, and shelter themselves. Additionally, parental love fosters the intellectual, spiritual, and emotional growth of children. Parental love most clearly reveals the primary paradox of love: the persons whom we love are gifts to us as much as we are gifts to them.

**Love of God.** Love begins with God's love for us, incarnated primarily in those who love us. Loving other people is the school in which we learn to love God. As Saint John said, "Those who say, 'I love God,' and hate their brothers or sisters, are liars; for those who do not love a brother or sister whom they have seen, cannot love God whom they have not seen" (1 John 4:20).

This God of infinite love invites us into relationship. Like any relationship, a relationship with God requires time and attention. We can attend to God and develop our love of God in two ways: loving other people and being with God in prayer and worship.

## Praying and Love

God floods us with the grace to love, but love demands much of us. So we often fail to love. Another translation of Paul's admonition to "Pursue love" is "Make love your aim." This translation highlights the relationship between love and sin. The word *sin* has its origins in a word meaning "to miss the mark." So while we aim at love, we often miss the mark.

We fail to love in many ways. We beat ourselves up for not meeting our goals, for carrying around an extra few pounds, or for not making enough money. We shy away from visiting a friend in the hospital because it's too painful. We start a fight with a friend over something trivial or because we are jealous about her or his accomplishments. We refuse to give donations to help the local food shelf resupply for the winter. We betray the trust of our beloved in a dozen small acts of disloyalty like refusing to share our feelings about perceived slights. We lash out at our teenage children or ignore them as much as possible. In short, we love, at best, imperfectly and at worst, not at all.

Thus we pray for love. In our desperate desire to correct our aim at loving wisely and well, we turn to God. We seek God's direction, energy, and presence with us. This plea for help is perfectly natural. Indeed, the root of the word *prayer* means "to obtain by entreaty." By asking God for help, we also remind ourselves of our deep desire to love.

Praying about love nourishes the seed of love that God has planted in our heart. Praying for love focuses our attention on how we love and who we love. Many of the problems we have in loving come from not paying attention, not listening, and not noticing. In the Hebrew Scriptures, when the Chosen People had fallen into sin, the prophets would begin their calls to conversion with, "Hear, O Israel" or "Listen." Meditating on the stories and passages in this book should help you listen to your heart, examine aspects of how you love, and plan loving moments in your imagination.

Praying about love invites us to celebrate and give thanks for the love that has been a gift to us. Remembering experiences of this gift not only warms our heart, but reminds us of love's place in our present life. When we celebrate love, we reinforce our resolve to care in the future.

## Aim for Love

We are compelled by our very nature to love and to seek love. The Christian vocation, or call, is to love. Loving is not simple. It challenges us in ways that call upon all our resources, but it also energizes us and brings us to life. All of us have much to learn about love. We are not meant to be perfect.

Even so, God has claimed us as lovable just as we are. If we believe in God's love for us, perhaps we will believe in our own ability to love. God's grace perpetually flows to us. And so we pray to accept the grace to love. May each of these thirty-one days of prayer for love challenge, invite, inspire, and inform us to love more fully, wisely, and well.

DAY 1

# *Let Us Love*

*Listen* Dear friends,

Let us love one another. The grace to love flows from God. Everyone who loves is a child of God. . . . God is love. Indeed, God loves us so much that God sent Jesus the Christ so that we might have full life through him. No human being has ever seen God but, when we love each other, God dwells in us and God's love comes to completion in us. . . . So put your faith in the love that God has for you. God is love. Since God loves us so incredibly, then we should love one another. . . . Let us love because God loved us first.

(1 John 4: 7–19)

■ ■ ■

*Reflect* We can love because the God who is love dwells within us, urging us to love, inviting us to love, and giving us the courage to love.

Consider, one by one, the many invitations that God has given you and continues to give you to love—in creation, from friends, family, and those who need help. A beloved's smile is an invitation to love; the wonder at the talents God has given us is an invitation to love; a child's cry is an invitation to love; and so is the sign worn by a homeless person saying, "Will work for food."

Thank God for each invitation to love.

*Respond* God, you are love, and your love makes it possible for me to love other people. In gratitude for your love, I say with Saint Ignatius:

> Take Lord, and receive all my liberty, my memory, my understanding, my entire will—all that I have and call my own. You have given it all to me. To you, Lord, I return it. Everything is yours; do with it what you will. Give me only your love and your grace. That is enough for me.

DAY 2

# *Created in God's Image*

*Listen* God said, "Let us make human beings in our own image, in the likeness of ourselves." . . . God created human beings in God's own image, in the image of God they were created, male and female God created them. . . . God blessed them. . . . And so it was, looking at all of Creation, God recognized it as very good.

(Genesis 1:26–31)

We are God's work of art, created in Christ Jesus for the good works which God has already designated to make up our way of life.

(Ephesians 2:10)

■ ■ ■

**Reflect** God declared us "good"; we are works of the Creator's art. We are created to reflect the power, wonder, and mystery of the Creator. All of us—no matter how short or tall, fat or thin, brilliant or intellectually challenged, athletic or studious—are made in the image of our Creator. When we love ourselves—respect, honor, develop, educate, appreciate, accept ourselves, and foster the good in us—we are showing our love and appreciation to God.

Ponder the gifts, talents, and skills—the wonder that you are as a person—and then thank God for each gift and the gift of your being.

**Respond** God, you know everything about me. You comprehend my feelings, thoughts, and intentions. You have observed my actions and know my body from the soles of my feet to the crown of my head. You created me, knitting me together in my mother's womb. For the wonder, beauty, and mystery of myself, I thank you, loving God. Help me to love myself as much as you love me.

(Psalm 139)

DAY 3

# *Why Were You Not Zusya?*

*Listen*

The old rabbi Zusya was the master of a group of disciples. One day he became ill, and within a week he was on his deathbed. His disciples gathered around him to pray the Psalms and comfort him in his dying moments.

As the end drew near, the disciples heard Zusya utter his last words: "In the next world, they will not ask of me, 'Why were you not *Moses?*' They will ask of me, 'Why were you not *Zusya?*'"

■ ■ ■

**Reflect**

Morality means returning to our core—that true center of who we really are as God created us—where we are fully human. However, we tend to evade our full humanity because we naturally seek to avoid the pain and grief that is part of being human. One way of evading our humanness is to try to be someone else: Moses instead of Zusya. The self we need to love is ourself, not someone else's self.

Reflect on any temptations you have to elude your humanity or to deny your unique manifestation of the Creator. How can you celebrate yourself?

**Respond**

Creative God, you made me one of a kind. Maybe I don't understand the reasons behind being the way I am, but help me accept, appreciate, and love myself. I don't want to show up on Judgment Day only to have you ask, "Why were you not [your name]?" Help me embrace myself, develop the me that you have made me to be, and learn to love fully as me and not someone else. After all, you only expect me to be me. May I be satisfied with that. You are.

DAY 4

# *Loving Our Body-Self*

## *Listen*

And when our soul is breathed into our body, at which time we are made sensual, at once mercy and grace begin to work, having care of us and protecting us with pity and love, in which operation the Holy Spirit forms in our faith the hope that we shall return up above to our substance, into the power of Christ, increased and fulfilled through the Holy Spirit. So I understand that our sensuality is founded in nature, in mercy and in grace, and this foundation enables us to receive gifts which lead us to endless life. For I saw very surely that our substance is in God, and I also saw that God is in our sensuality, for in the same instant and place in which our soul is made sensual, in that same instant and place exists the city of God, ordained for him from without beginning. He comes into this city and will never depart from it, for God is never out of the soul, in which he will dwell blessedly without end.

(Julian of Norwich)

■ ■ ■

## Reflect

The holy mystic Julian understood that God made us as whole creations: body and soul. God comes to us in our body and soul. Love of God does not require negation of our bodiliness, our sensuality. In Julian's spirituality, our substance and sensuality together may rightly be called our soul, and our experience of God can be expressed in and through our body. Christian self-love requires that we love, care for, and cherish our body as well as our spirit.

Reflect on the wonder of your body, the marvel of its quiet, efficient functioning, and the ways it enables you to care for other people, and enjoy God's creation. Thank God for your body-self.

## Respond

God, you gave me my body for loving, enjoying, and serving. Help me to embrace my body-self and to treat it as your "temple . . . with the Spirit of God living" in it (1 Corinthians 3:16–17). Grant me the grace to reject all the messages that tell me my body is ugly, inadequate, unfashionable, and so on. May I treat it like your "work of art" (Ephesians 2:10). May I celebrate my body-self by sensing the wonders of your creation, giving love, and enjoying the fullness of life. For my body, thank you, my Creator.

DAY 5

# *The Paradox of Self-Love*

## *Listen*

We cannot love ourselves unless we love others, and we cannot love others unless we love ourselves. But a selfish love of ourselves makes us incapable of loving others. The difficulty of this commandment lies in the paradox that it would have us love ourselves unselfishly, because even our love of ourselves is something we owe to others. . . .

We do not exist for ourselves alone, and it is only when we are fully convinced of this fact that we begin to love ourselves properly and thus also love others. What do I mean by loving ourselves properly? I mean, first of all, desiring to live, accepting life as a very great gift and a great good, not because of what it gives us, but because of what it enables us to give to others. . . .

If we live for others, we will gradually discover that no one expects us to be "as gods." We will see that we are human, like everyone else, that we all have weaknesses and deficiencies, and that these limitations of ours play a most important part in all our lives. It is because of them that we need others and others need us. We are not all weak in the same spots, and so we supplement and complete one another.

(Thomas Merton)

■ ■ ■

## *Reflect*

As with many aspects of life, self-love is paradoxical. We love ourselves so that we can love other people; we accept, even embrace, our limitations and weaknesses precisely because they urge us to reach out to other people and enter into relationships.

Reflect on your experience of weakness leading to love and accepting your own life as a "great good" leading to a stronger desire to love.

## *Respond*

God of wisdom and wonder, grant that I may perceive my weaknesses and limitations as "happy faults" that prompt me to extend my hand to other people. Inflame me with a desire to live fully, to give thanks and praise for the gift of life, and to share my gifts with other people. Help me to keep the paradox clearly in my heart that I cannot love myself without loving others, and I cannot love others without loving myself. Blessed be you, all-wise and wonderful God.

DAY 6

# *The Returns of Love*

## *Listen*

The women at the shelter knew I was new, and one of them enjoyed giving me a hard time about it. Despite this, we became close friends, and it was much to my dismay that I returned to work one afternoon and discovered she had moved out unexpectedly. Not getting a chance to say good-bye is a part of the job I have not become used to.

A few days later, I came across her file. When women leave the shelter, they are asked to answer some questions. In response to "My favorite thing about . . ." this woman had written "the staff—especially Kelly!" I didn't know whether to laugh or to cry. I miss her.

(Kelly Smith)

■ ■ ■

*Reflect* Love is an I-Thou relationship in which both people greet each other's souls. This is what happened to Kelly Smith in an unexpected way while working as a volunteer in a shelter for battered women. Kelly soul-greeted one of her clients, and the compliment was returned.

Recall experiences when your self-love was affirmed by giving love to someone else. Give thanks for these experiences and ask God for the grace to soul-greet.

*Respond* God of surprises, affirmations of our self-worth, our competence, ourselves can come from unexpected sources. Grant me courage to act with charity to people around me, especially those most in need. May I cease worrying about receiving something back and trust that charity is its own reward. Then, gracious God, when someone does affirm me, I will be doubly blessed and gifted.

DAY 7

# *The Treasure of Friendship*

*Listen*

Faithful friends are a sturdy
shelter:
whoever finds one has found a
treasure.
Faithful friends are beyond price;
no amount can balance their
worth.
Faithful friends are life-saving
medicine;
and those who fear [God]
will find them.
Those who fear [God] direct
their friendship aright,
for as they are, so are their
neighbors also.

(Ecclesiasticus 6:14–17)

■ ■ ■

***Reflect*** Bible stories offer famous friendships as models: David and Jonathan, Ruth and Naomi. Friends are our support, defense, life givers, and mentors. They are blessings from a gracious God.

Bring to mind each of your true friends: those who support and defend you, who nurture your life energy and mentor you, who offer you truth to win your trust. Hold them in your attention and cherish their goodness. Then thank God for each one.

***Respond*** Holy Friend, bless you for the gift of friends. Alone I am vulnerable, sometimes helpless, and lonely. My friends show me your love, share their energy and joy in life, and draw me to goodness. Bless my friends. Grant that I may love them as wisely and well as they love me.

DAY 8

# A Friend Indeed

## *Listen*

Two friends were traveling together when a bear suddenly appeared. One of them climbed up a tree in time and remained there hidden. The other, seeing that he would be caught in another moment, lay down on the ground and pretended to be dead. When the bear put its muzzle to him and smelt him all over, he held his breath—for it is said that a bear will not touch a corpse. After it had gone away, the other man came down from his tree and asked his friend what the bear had whispered in his ear. "It told me," he replied, "not to travel in future with friends who do not stand by one in peril."

Genuine friends are proved by adversity.

(Aesop)

■ ■ ■

## Reflect

Columnist Walter Winchell said that "a friend is someone who walks in when the rest of the world walks out." True friends will not desert us when the going gets rough. Lots of "bears" threaten us and our friends: small acts of betrayal, family breakups, and broken promises. Part of any loving relationship is loyalty in adversity.

Bring to mind times when adversity has showed who your true friends are, and then thank God for the loyalty of those friends.

## Respond

Holy Friend, despite our sins against you and one another, you never deserted us. Instead, you sent Jesus to be our savior, to teach us how to love one another, and to show us how to be true friends. Loyal love cost Jesus his life. May I be a loyal friend. Grant me courage and faithfulness. Thank you for your friendship and that of my loyal, true friends.

DAY 9

# The Harmony of Equals

## Listen

Friendship is an equality made of harmony. . . . There is equality because each wishes to preserve the faculty of free consent both in himself and in the other.

When anyone wishes to put himself under a human being or consents to be subordinated to him, there is no trace of friendship. . . . There is no friendship where there is inequality. . . .

In a perfect friendship, . . . two friends have fully consented to be two and not one, they respect the distance which the fact of being two distinct creatures places between them. Man has the right to desire direct union with God alone.

Friendship is a miracle by which a person consents to view from a certain distance, and without coming any nearer, the very being who is necessary to him as food.

(Simone Weil)

■ ■ ■

**Reflect** Friendship, to be genuine, needs to be a two-way street. We give and receive mutually over time and through various ways, equally. In a mutual and equal friendship, two friends will each initiate getting together, will each talk about where to go for lunch rather than one deciding all the time, will each give gifts to the other without being reminded, and will tell each other what is on one's mind and in one's heart, so that what is known about one is equal with what the other knows.

Reflect on the miracle of equality in your friendships. Do you have a friend with whom you want to create more harmony or equality?

**Respond** Holy Friend, maintaining harmony and equality in friendship can be an enormous challenge. Sometimes my ego gets in the way. I want to take control or be taken care of. In my heart I know that I need true friends with whom I can share equally in the matters of our hearts, the joy of living, the tasks to be done, and the problems to be dealt with. Teach me how to be sensitive to harmony, balance, and equality.

DAY 10

# *Sacrifice*

## *Listen*

I had just broken up with my fiancé. I found out he was running around with one of my best friends. I was livid and so deeply hurt. Then Brian called. I started blubbering and then ranting and raving, not my usual confident self at all. So he drove down from San Francisco—about an hour's drive. It was like nine at night when he had called.

Anyway, he got there about 10:30. I went through my whole crying, ranting, hurt, angry tirade. Used up a box of Kleenex and must have drenched the shoulder of his shirt. He just hugged me when I needed it, listened, agreed that my ex was a jerk and my friend just as bad. Well, by the time I finished getting the whole mess out, I was exhausted, but felt much relieved. He left at 3:00 a.m. and had to work the next day.

I hate to think what I would have done if Brian hadn't come. There's nothing like that physical presence of someone who I know cares for me. I'd do the same for Brian, but I'll always be grateful. Anyway, I sent him gift certificates for the butter-brickle ice cream he adores; I owe him a lot more, but friends like us don't need huge things to say thanks with.

■ ■ ■

*Reflect* A friend may make a detour on a trip just to spend a half hour with her or his friend, take the other to a job interview when his or her car breaks down, and lend favorite clothes. Friends also confront us with caring honesty at the risk of our anger. Friendship, like any love, sometimes means sacrificing and risking for the larger good of helping a friend.

Recall times when friends have sacrificed for you and when you have risked for them.

*Respond* Generous God, you certainly showed us how to sacrifice for love and to risk the truth. You sent Jesus to us. He wandered the roads of Palestine—healing, listening, and telling the Good News. He never had a place to lay his head that he could call his own. Jesus called us friends. Of course, he made the ultimate sacrifice for us. When I shrink from the sacrifices sometimes demanded by friendship, may I be inspired by Christ's example and be graced by the power of your Spirit. Help me become a willing friend.

DAY 11

# *Destined for Friendship*

## *Listen*

The truth remains that our destiny is to love one another as Christ has loved us. Jesus . . . is to every soul born into the world, that soul's most intimate friend. The lives of all . . . we meet and know are woven into our own destiny, together with the lives of many we shall never know on earth. But certain ones, very few, are our close friends. Because we have more in common with them, we are able to love them with a special selfless perfection, since we have more to share. They are inseparable from our own destiny, and, therefore, our love for them is especially holy: it is a manifestation of God in our lives.

(Thomas Merton)

■ ■ ■

## *Reflect*

In Hosea 11:1–4, God speaks about loving sinful and ungrateful Israel: "'I led them with cords of human kindness, with bands of love.'" God does the same with us. People who love us show us the face of our loving God in a way that we can understand. They lead us "with bands of love" to a meeting with God. Thus, friends play an indispensable role in our destiny to be totally and finally united with our Creator.

How have your friends led you "with cords of human kindness, with bands of love" back to God? How do you do the same for them?

## *Respond*

Divine Friend, you send me friends for support, affirmation, challenge, and consolation. But you also grace me with friends who will always lead me back to you. May I always acknowledge that the love of my friends is a manifestation of your love for me and a foretaste of the final loving union you desire for me. Help me to respond to the love of my friends with a generous, hopeful heart.

DAY 12

# *Friends of Differing Gifts*

*Listen* My best friend, Bill, identifies with my career. If I take a beating on a book, Bill is right by my side. He's on my team. He'll threaten to punch out a critic or he'll say, "Come on, let's ride up in the Blue Ridge and forget these turkeys." [My men friends] will go out of their way to introduce me to people they think could help me. . . . Most of them are able to draw closer to me through an activity. In other words, we usually don't sit and chat, we do something. . . . I need my men friends. I learn something from them that I can't learn from women, namely, what it is like to be a man.

(Rita Mae Brown)

*Reflect* A bit of management wisdom can apply to friendship: "If we agree on everything, one of us isn't needed." Friends with differing gifts bring a terrific richness to a relationship. Musician friends invite those of us who are "tune challenged" to enjoy the wonders of melody and the passions of harmony. Our outdoor friends show us the beauty of finches and the marvels of swamps. Friends of differing gifts are pearls of great price.

Bring to mind how your friends bring differing but marvelous gifts to you. Have you denied yourself pleasures

■ ■ ■

and possibilities because you did not cultivate friendships with those you perceived as different?

## *Respond*

God, you created women and men to dance together in joy and hope and gave us friends of various talents and personalities so that we can learn from and cherish one another. May we always remember the words of this poem and celebrate friendship between ourselves and friends of differing gifts:

> "I" is such a slender word,
> a selfish word.
> "We" is broader and enchanting
> for it doubles the outlook.
>
> (Mary Paquette)

Amen to friendship. Thanks be to you, Holy Friend.

DAY 13

# *Love's Light*

## *Listen*

Sunset: a cloud the color of your skin
When luminous with river water, bare.
Above, a sky steadily turning blue
That soon will be as live-black as your hair.

Light alters day. Love alters us. We are
The woman and the man each knew before,
But changed by love's abruptness, as a dark
Room burns with sunlight from an opened door.

(Paul Engle)

■ ■ ■

***Reflect*** Love alters us by giving us light to see into the darknesses in our life. The light of love can turn despair into hope, ignorance into understanding, and icy loneliness into warm embracing. The light cast by love may illumine painful areas of our life that were long hidden by denial or neglect.

Reflect on the light that love has brought into your life. How has a loved one helped you to view and appreciate parts of your life that might have been painful and hidden?

***Respond*** You are the light of the world, living God. Your love, shining from loved ones, cuts through the darkness, turning night into day. May I step boldly into this light of love, be warmed by it, and follow it through my fears and doubts. Whenever the sun rises, or a candle flickers, or a lamp illumines a shadowy room, may I recall your love, burning from those who love me. All glory to you, Light of my Life.

DAY 14

# *Entwined*

*Listen* A portion of your soul has been
entwined with mine.
A gentle kind of togetherness, while
separately we stand.
As two trees deeply rooted in
separate plots of ground,
While their topmost branches
come together,
Forming a miracle of lace
against the heavens.

(Janet Miles)

■ ■ ■

## Reflect

One of the wonders and paradoxes of love between two people is that while their souls and bodies, hearts and minds may be entwined, their unique and separate souls remain inviolate. Indeed, they are enhanced. Such love creates a miracle.

Share your thoughts and feelings with the Creator of this miracle. Tell our Divine Lover about the miracle of the love you share with a beloved.

## Respond

God of all creation,
You call us to love,
to become entwined with our beloved.
Lead us to understand in our heart
what the Song of Songs says,

> What spells lie in . . . love. . . .
> How delicious is . . . love, more delicious than wine!
> (Song of Songs 4:10)

Amen. Alleluia!

DAY 15

# *The Kiss*

*Listen* I stand by the bed where the young woman lies . . . her face, postoperative . . . her mouth twisted in palsy . . . clownish. A tiny twig of the facial nerve, one of the muscles of her mouth, has been severed. She will be that way from now on. I had followed with religious fervor the curve of her flesh, I promise you that. Nevertheless, to remove the tumor in her cheek, I had cut this little nerve. Her young husband is in the room. He stands on the opposite side of the bed, and together they seem to be in a world all their own in the evening lamplight . . . isolated from me . . . private.

Who are they? I ask myself . . . he and this wry mouth I have made, who gaze at and touch each other so generously. The young woman speaks. "Will my mouth always be like this?" she asks. "Yes," I say, "it will. It is because the nerve was cut." She nods and is silent. But the young man smiles. "I like it," he says. "It's kind of cute."

All at once I know who he is. I understand, and I lower my gaze. One is not bold in an encounter with the divine. Unmindful, he bends to kiss her crooked mouth, and I am

■ ■ ■

so close I can see how he twists his own lips to accommodate to hers . . . to show her that their kiss still works.

(Richard Selzer)

*Reflect*

Richard Selzer, a surgeon, encountered divine love in these two people. The young husband's love is godly because, like God's love, it is accepting, affirming, accommodating, and generously affectionate. Love is about our souls, not our upholstery. Love between two people mirrors to us all the infinite, unconditional love of God. These moments of love form the "'bands of love'" (Hosea 11:4) that God uses to lead us into the divine embrace.

Ask yourself: How flexible, accommodating, and accepting am I with one I love?

*Respond*

Affectionate, loving God, help me to love, accept, affirm, and accommodate my beloved as beautifully as the young man did his wife. Strengthen the bonds of our love so that all people will know that your love lives on in the great sacrament of love between two human beings. May all my actions be like the young man's kiss, the loving sign of our commitment to one another. Bless you, loving God, for such love. May it come to full flower in us.

DAY 16

# We Will It So

*Listen*

By our wills,
we transform
to live together.

. . . . . . . . . . . .

At our age the imagination
across the sorry facts
lifts us
to make roses
stand before thorns.

. . . . . . . . . . . .

But we are older,

. . . . . . . . . . . .

we have
no matter how,
by our wills survived
to keep
the jeweled prize
always at our finger tips.
We will it so
and so it is
past all accident.

(William Carlos Williams)

■ ■ ■

**Reflect** Williams reminds us that two people who love each other have to "will it so . . . past all accident." Love grows with flowers and thorns. Only steady purpose, a clear eye on reality, a vital imagination, and persistence can help two lovers see the rose past the thorns. Long love is not an accident. In fact, all love requires us to see the rose past the thorns.

Ponder the ways your imagination and will have helped your love blossom into roses, even amid the thorns. How has your beloved or those you love helped you to "will it so"?

**Respond** Living God, willing love may seem rather cold, but I know differently. In the hard times with ones I love, I have to "will it so . . . past all accident." Grace me with imagination to see the roses and courage to transform my will so that we can keep the "jeweled prize" of love alive and growing. Daffodils, like young love, spring up miraculously, but disappear all too quickly. Make our love a sturdy rosebush that keeps blossoming all season, year after year.

DAY 17

# *You Mad Lover, You*

## *Listen*

After all these years,
who would have thought
we'd last?
Gray in my hair,
and reformed by the years,
I've learned to love you
in the most unusual ways—
plowing gardens,
balancing budgets,
going to City Council,
and picking up garbage
with public housing residents.

. . . . . . . . . . . . . . . . .

Come,
you say,
and once again I regret
how late I came to love you
and come running, drawn by you to the world.

(Theresa Johnson)

■ ■ ■

## Reflect

We often learn to love in ways we never expected, just as Theresa Johnson suggests. Large and important tasks or the most mundane duties can draw two people together if they let them. Each event becomes a peek into the character of each other and a thing accomplished together. Love like this draws us "to the world." Christlike love leads us to love more widely, openly, and generously.

Reflect on ways your beloved or those you love have called you to love other people, to serve your neighbors, and to cherish creation? Thank the people you love for expanding your ability to love.

## Respond

God, love is a divine madness. It leads me down paths that never would have tempted me before. It feels like madness when I realize that I cannot control a loved one's affection for me, or regulate their desires and hopes for the future. Yet I join the dance, and my love and I put our shoulders to the same wheel, join hands, and walk forward. Love draws me out into the world. You planned this divine madness. I thank you for the adventure, the energy, and the hope. May I continue to be a mad lover!

DAY 18

# *Like Your Own Body*

*Listen*

Mary sat watching [Rosicky] intently, trying to find any change in his face. It is hard to see anyone who has become like your own body to you. Yes, his hair had got thin, and his high forehead had deep lines running from left to right. . . . He was shorter and broader than when she married him; his back had grown broad and curved, a good deal like the shell of an old turtle. . . .

He was fifteen years older than Mary, but she hardly ever thought about it before. He was her man, and the kind of man she liked. . . . They had been shipmates on a rough voyage and had stood by each other in trying times. Life had gone well with them because, at bottom, they had the same ideas about life. . . . It was as if they had thought the same thought together. . . . Though he had married a rough farm girl, he had never touched her without gentleness.

(Willa Cather)

■ ■ ■

## *Reflect*

Hard times make a couple like Mary and Rosicky "shipmates on a rough voyage" who know that they can count on one another. Their love may not be glamorous, too demonstrative, or sweetly romantic, but it has the strength of deep roots that sustain and bring fresh greenness just when it should. They have a fundamental trust that knows that nothing is as strong as gentleness or as gentle as strength.

Recall any couple you know who have lived and loved through long years. Ponder what they teach you about loving. Give thanks for them.

## *Respond*

God of the good times and the hard times, grant me the courage, patience, openness, and flexibility to love my beloved through the winters and springs of our relationship, all during the heat of summer, and into the fall. Instruct my heart and soul in gentleness and understanding. When our ship is tossed by stormy seas, grant us the grace to sustain each other, and then guide us to calmer waters where we can patch up our canvas, clear the decks, and reset our course.

DAY 19

# *By Mercy Judged*

*Listen* The Corporal Works are to feed the hungry, to give drink to the thirsty, to clothe the naked, to ransom the captive, to harbor the harborless, to visit the sick, and to bury the dead. . . .

The Works of Mercy are a wonderful stimulus to our growth in faith as well as love. Our faith is taxed to the utmost and so grows through this strain put upon it. It is pruned again and again, and springs up bearing much fruit. For anyone starting to live literally the words of the Fathers of the Church—"The bread you retain belongs to the hungry, the dress you lock up is the property of the naked"; "What is superfluous for one's need is to be regarded as plunder if one retains it for one's self"—there is always a trial ahead. "Our faith, more precious than gold, must be tried as though by fire."

It is by the Works of Mercy that we shall be judged.

(Dorothy Day)

■ ■ ■

*Reflect* The works of mercy are the first acts of justice and the first steps toward love. The corporal works of mercy are named by Jesus as the criteria—the bottom line—for entrance into the Reign of God.

Imagine yourself in the judgment scene, standing before Christ. Jesus asks you these questions and you respond to each one:

- "Did you feed the hungry?"
- "Did you visit the sick or imprisoned?"
- "Did you give refreshing drink to the thirsty?"
- "Did you clothe the naked?"
- "Did you make room for strangers?"

*Respond* Merciful God, teach me love for all your people, but teach me especially to bring your love to the hungry, sick, imprisoned, thirsty, homeless, and strangers. Grant that I may then say with the psalmist:

> Happy those who aid the poor and the lowly.
> God will help them when they are in trouble.
> Yahweh will protect and preserve them,
> will make them happy in the land.
>
> (Psalm 41:1–2)

DAY 20

# *Do Something*

*Listen*

One day, as usually was the case, a young waif, a little girl, stood at the street corner begging for food, money, or whatever she could get. Now this girl was wearing very tattered clothes; she was dirty and quite disheveled.

As it happens, a well-to-do young man passed that corner without giving the girl a second look. But when he returned to his expensive home, his happy and comfortable family, and his well-laden dinner table, his thoughts returned to the young waif and he became very angry at God for allowing such conditions to exist.

He reproached God, saying, "How can you let this happen? Why don't you do something to help this girl?"

Then he heard God in the depths of his being respond by saying, "I did. I created you!"

(Anonymous)

■ ■ ■

**Reflect**

God's love is not romantic; it is manifest through human hands, like ours. The Gospel challenges us to pray and act.

Ask yourself: How do I manifest God's love to people in need through my actions as well as in my prayers? Consider people close at hand in your family, among your neighbors, or the people you work with, as well as needy people in distant lands.

**Respond**

God of mercy and compassion, may I love in my words and in my deeds. When I come up with excuses or try to blame you for the world's ills, call me from the depths of my heart to charity. Remind me as you reminded the young man in the story that you sent me to be your love to the hungry, sick, homeless, thirsty, and imprisoned. Grant me the grace of courage, honesty, and faith so that I may love as you love.

DAY 21

# Secret Meeting

*Listen*

It intrigued the congregation to see their rabbi disappear each week on the eve of the Sabbath. They suspected he was secretly meeting the Almighty, so they deputed one of their number to follow him.

This is what the man saw: the rabbi disguised himself in peasant clothes and served a paralyzed Gentile woman in her cottage, cleaning out the room and preparing a Sabbath meal for her.

When the spy got back, the congregation asked, "Where did the rabbi go? Did he ascend to heaven?"

"No," the man replied, "he went even higher."

(Anthony de Mello)

■ ■ ■

**Reflect** All the major religions of the world place compassionate love at the center of their morality. Charity offers us a chance to meet and to serve God face-to-face. What makes the rabbi's love so remarkable is that he served a Gentile woman. Like the good Samaritan of the Christian Scriptures, the rabbi's love cut through prejudices and social constrictions. "He went even higher," and it was his charity that took him there.

Reflect on the story and its challenges for you.

**Respond** Kindly, compassionate God, may I ascend even higher by acting with charity toward anyone who needs my aid. Like the holy rabbi, may I act lovingly without fanfare and recognition, or even the approval of others. May I love generously, wisely, and steadily. O You who are love, guide me to place love at the center of my living.

DAY 22

# *Jesus the Poor*

## *Listen*

Let us . . . cherish the poor as our masters, since Our Lord is in them and they in Our Lord. . . .

Let us love God, . . . let us love God. But let it be with the strength of our arms and the sweat of our brow. . . .

So very often, many outpourings of affection for God, of resting in his presence, of good feelings toward everyone and sentiments and prayers like these, although very good and very desirable, are nonetheless suspect if they do not express themselves in practical love which has real effects. . . .

We must pass . . . from affective love to effective love. And that is a love which takes flesh in works of charity, service of the poor which is undertaken with joy, constancy and tender love.

(Vincent de Paul)

■ ■ ■

## Reflect

For a person like Vincent de Paul, the poor were indeed his masters because he took Christ at his word: "'Just as you did [a work of mercy] to one of the least of these who are members of my family, you did it to me'" (Matthew 25:40). In serving those in need, Vincent—and we—serve God. This service needs to be both from the heart and "effective love."

Reflect on people who challenge you to see God in them. How can you love them in heart and in deed? Pray to know how to love them.

## Respond

Loving God, may I see your presence in sick, imprisoned, or suffering people. Change my ways of seeing; then strengthen my will to act with justice and charity. Today, I pray especially for . . .

DAY 23

# The Faith to Love

## *Listen*

A family of five were enjoying their day at the beach. The children were bathing in the ocean and making castles in the sand when in the distance a little old lady appeared. Her gray hair was blowing in the wind and her clothes were dirty and ragged. She was muttering something to herself as she picked up things from the beach and put them into a bag.

The parents called the children to their side and told them to stay away from the old lady. As she passed by, bending down every now and then to pick things up, she smiled at the family. But her greeting wasn't returned.

Many weeks later they learned that the little old lady had made it her lifelong crusade to pick up bits of glass from the beach so children wouldn't cut their feet.

(Anthony de Mello)

■ ■ ■

*Reflect* Just because we are loving does not mean that people will understand or appreciate us and what we do. Jesus suffered the same fate. His acts of compassionate love were greeted with jealousy, anger, and mistrust. Has fear of being misunderstood ever kept you away from acting compassionately? Have you ever experienced misunderstanding because of your love? Talk with God about this.

*Respond* God, your son, Jesus, suffered because of his loving care of sick, poor, and outcast people. Grant me courage to act with love even in the face of mistrust and fear. May I have the faith and courage to keep picking up the broken glass even when I am greeted with suspicion. No one told us that love would be easy. I just need your help to keep trying.

DAY 24

# Never Too Late

## Listen

It is no use saying that we are born two thousand years too late to give room to Christ. Nor will those who live at the end of the world have been born too late. Christ is always with us, always asking for room in our hearts. . . .

All that the friends of Christ did for Him in his lifetime, we can do. Peter's mother-in-law hastened to cook a meal for Him, and if anything in the Gospels can be inferred, it surely is that she gave the very best she had, with no thought of extravagance. . . .

The people of Samaria, despised and isolated, were overjoyed to give Him hospitality, and for days He walked and ate and slept among them. And the loveliest of all relationships in Christ's life, after His relationship with His Mother, is His friendship with Martha, Mary, and Lazarus and the continual hospitality He found with them. . . .

We can do it too, exactly as they did. We are not born too late. We do it by seeing Christ and serving Christ in friends and strangers, in everyone we come in contact with. . . .

He made heaven hinge on the way we act toward Him in His disguise of commonplace, frail, ordinary humanity.

(Dorothy Day)

■ ■ ■

*Reflect* Each day is a chance to offer and receive compassion. All of time is sacred time, Christ time. Pray the experiences of the last twenty-four hours. Talk to God about how you served your sisters and brothers and how they served you.

*Respond* God of charity, you offer us infinite hospitality. May I return this same hospitality to "commonplace, frail, ordinary humanity." Each person is holy; each stranger sacred. I desire an attitude of welcome and joyful gratitude. Lead me to offer what I have to give—openly, warmly, and generously. All blessings, praise, and thanks to you, hospitable, wonderful God.

DAY 25

# *Fed by Love*

## *Listen*

I've always treasured 2:00 a.m. feedings. It seemed to be the only time that I got to hold my baby without having to divide my time between the other children. . . .

One night as I sat in the dark of my living room holding the baby that had fallen asleep at my breast, I marveled at the gift of life. This gift of life given to me. This child, so fragile, so dependent, is loved unconditionally simply because he exists. He grew in my womb and was brought forth in living water, making me so vulnerable, making me see life brand new all over again. . . .

I began a dialog with God. I knew in my head that God's love was even more perfect than mine. . . . Two o'clock became a sacramental moment, for I was able to see that the child asleep in my lap was a perfect container for God's love. To look at the face of God and know God's love would be too awesome for me to handle. In the image of my child I could safely encounter the unconditional love of God. . . .

At the 2:00 a.m. feeding, I was being fed. Sometimes between the dark of night and the light of day I was called

■ ■ ■

by name, and I came to know what it means to be a daughter of God.

(Karen DeFilippis)

## Reflect

In feeding her baby, in holding and nurturing this child, Karen is fed and nurtured by the loving God. All love comes from God; to give love draws us closer to the source of all love.

No matter how old you are, close your eyes and imagine yourself being held by the warm, radiant hands of God. What does it feel like? Now recall a time when you gave nurturing love to a child or to someone who needed it. How did that feel? How was God drawing you closer?

## Respond

All praise and blessings to you, God who is love, for the power to nurture and feed, to shelter and protect those who cannot do these things for themselves. Thank you for the grace to encounter you in the process of loving. Bless the children who grace me with their trust, their needs, and the chance to serve. May any act of love that you give me the grace to do be the seed of more generous charity. Please, God, may we keep meeting in acts of love.

DAY 26

# *Nurturing Love*

## *Listen*

Silly. All giggles and ringlets and never
about to stop anything without fussing:
get down I say! Do you think I took your mother
to beget me a chimp for my shoulder?
I'm forty, boy, and no weight lifter.
Go find some energy your own size.
Get down!—Well, just once more.
There. Now get down, you baby-fat incubus.
Go ride your imagination. No, I don't care
how many kisses you'll write me a check for.
A million? Some banker you are. Still—
a million of anything is a lot of something.
All right. Once more, then. But just once. You hear?

(John Ciardi)

■ ■ ■

## Reflect

Children sometimes seem to demand more energy, patience, affection, and attention than we can give, but they also engage our playfulness and give us joy. Joy allows us to forgive our failures as parents each night and begin again each morning learning to be better parents.

Reflect on your experiences of nurturing love both as receiver and giver. Talk with the Creator about the wonder and challenges of nurturing love.

## Respond

God, source of all nurturing, teach me to love your children. Jesus called the children to him and challenged all adults to care for them. Grant me the sensitivity, playfulness, wisdom, and patient strength to love children—to exercise my adult power for their greatest good. May their purity of heart and great neediness call forth all my generosity and goodness of spirit. Send us joy.

DAY 27

# *To My Children*

*Listen*

My neighbor said that while we were at Grandma's house
in California for a month,
it was like the neighborhood closed down for a while.
Now that you have left,
my heart has closed down.
I didn't expect it to do that.
I looked forward to the quiet,
to the milk cap staying on the jug,
to the front door remaining closed;
I wanted a night when I could watch
whatever I wanted on TV.
You called and said you were having lots of fun
and that Daddy's new wife was really nice,
and I said good.
When I hung up, I wept for your joy and my losses.

(Elizabeth Alexander)

■ ■ ■

## *Reflect*

Like night means day, love means loss. Sometimes we hunger for surcease of caring. We want the burdens of love to be forever light and yet have the full intimacy of loving. For better or worse, we cannot have it both ways.

Have you ever had an experience like Alexander's? How can you celebrate and embrace the weight of loving in your life?

## *Respond*

God, my divine parent, is this what Christ meant by taking up my cross to follow him? Sometimes the responsibilities of loving seem just too many to bear. Yet, I dread the suggestion that I could lose such love, such intimate sharing of life. God give me the courage, patience, and faith to carry on joyfully, hopefully, and generously. I especially need grace right now in dealing with . . .

DAY 28

# All We Can Do Is Suffer With

## Listen

Britain's Derek Redmond had dreamed all his life of winning a gold medal in the 400-meter race, and his dream was in sight as the gun sounded in the semifinals at [the] Barcelona [Olympics of 1992]. He was running the race of his life and could see the finish line as he rounded the turn into the backstretch. Suddenly he felt a sharp pain go up the back of his leg. He fell face first onto the track with a torn right hamstring.

*Sports Illustrated* recorded the dramatic events:

As the medical attendants were approaching, Redmond fought to his feet. . . . He set out hopping, in a crazed attempt to finish the race. When he reached the stretch, a large man in a T-shirt came out of the stands, hurled aside a security guard and ran to Redmond, embracing him. It was Jim Redmond, Derek's father. "You don't have to do this," he told his weeping son. "Yes, I do," said Derek. "Well, then," said Jim, "we're going to finish this together."

And they did. . . . The son's head sometimes buried in his father's shoulder, they stayed in Derek's lane all the way to the end, as the crowd gaped, then rose and howled and wept.

(Wayne Rice)

■ ■ ■

## Reflect

No matter how much parents love their children, they cannot always save them from pain and suffering. Often the only way for them to show love is to stay with their children in the midst of their pain. Compassion means to "suffer with." Jim Redmond's love for his son could not win the race for him or even take away the pain, but he could suffer with him. Love often calls for this kind of compassion.

Ponder the story and ask yourself: How has love of my children or others called me to be compassionate?

## Respond

God, teach me compassion. When those I love suffer, especially the children, I want to fix matters, stop the pain, rush in, and get things under control. Often I cannot. But I can walk with them, stand by them, and suffer with them. Help me realize that compassion is one way of loving, even if sometimes it is the hardest way of all. In particular, I need compassion in this situation . . .

DAY 29

# *New Horizons*

## *Listen*

You're a woman now, my daughter,
I can see it in your eyes
Feel it in your enthusiasm.
Your world is no longer
bounded by ours.
It stretches out
to new horizons
with pathways
of your choosing.
Go quickly now
else I'm too tempted
to call you back
to continue the interweaving
of twenty beautiful years.
But
when you're free
come back—
come back as my friend
so that
our worlds can meet
at the intersection
of love
and respect.

(Jean Spencer)

■ ■ ■

**Reflect** One painful element of parental love is letting go. After all the years of supporting, directing, correcting, and comforting, after all the tears and laughter, anger and tenderness, children need to step out and embrace adulthood. At this moment love means letting go, but hoping that the worlds will intersect.

Reflect on your own need to move away from family. If you have children, what grace do you need to be able to let go out of love?

**Respond** God of all growing, letting go of my loved ones has a bitter sweetness about it. I want them to stand on their own two feet, to come to the fullness of who they are, and to grow beyond even me. Plant hope deep in my soul that my love for them will always be a standing invitation for us to embrace each other out of need if it comes to that, but out of the freedom of people who love one another. Heal my fears for them, and . . . hold them in the palm of your hand.

DAY 30

# *Love Breeds Love*

## *Listen*

Dear Lord, you never tell us to do what is impossible . . . ; if, then, you tell me to love my sisters as you love them, that must mean that you yourself go on loving them in and through me—you know it wouldn't be possible in any other way. There would have been no new commandment, if you hadn't meant to give me the grace to keep it; how I welcome it, then, as proof that your will is to love, in and through me, all the people you tell me to love!

Always, when I act as charity bids, I have this feeling that it is Jesus who is acting in me; the closer my union with him, the greater my love for all. . . .

Love breeds love. . . . Love you as you love me? The only way to do that is to come to you [Jesus] for the loan of your own love; I couldn't content myself with less.

(Thérèse of Lisieux)

■ ■ ■

## *Reflect*

Love is not the result of personal achievement, but of complete availability to God's grace, so that charity, friendship, and affection are God's love flowing through us.

Pray a litany of thanks for the times when you have felt God's love flowing through you to other people. For instance, you might compose your litany like this: "For letting me console Maria yesterday at the funeral of her mother, I thank you, God who is love."

## *Respond*

"Love breeds love," Thérèse says. You, God, are love and you breed love in me and in anyone who asks. "Loan" me your love so that I can embrace all my sisters and brothers with your kindness, affection, attention, respect, charity, and wisdom. Love is such an enormous challenge that only your enormous grace makes it possible. Fill me with abundant love and then give me a generous spirit to let this love flow forth.

DAY 31

# *Loving God, Lover God*

*Listen* I came to India so I could love God. I wanted to work with the poor, work hard, and live a simple life. I felt like India was where God wanted me to be. . . .

I am here in India, and I have been loving God. The last two months I've been caring for abandoned babies and children with the Missionaries of Charity in Jamshedpur. . . . Feeding the little boy whose mother died when he was born, if only he could sit still then this rice and dal wouldn't be all over his face. . . .

I am here in India, and I think I've been loving God. Working with the poor. In the last two months, four babies have died and one is blind because of poor nutrition and disease. Working hard. Standing on my feet much of the day, sitting on the hard floor the rest of the day, catching colds and lice from the children, and changing all those diapers. . . .

I came to India because I thought that this was how I could love God. I knew India was a right thing, but my understanding was all wrong. Really I didn't come here to love God like I thought, coming here wasn't even my decision. God brought me here, India has been God's gift to me.

I now understand the reason I am in India is to learn how to let God love me.

(Laura Thomas)

*Reflect* As the Scriptures say, we love God by loving our neighbors as ourselves. We cannot love God whom we cannot see if we do not love our sisters and brothers whom we do see (1 John 4:20–21). When God offers us opportunities to love other people, God is really inviting us to share in divine love. In loving, we learn how to let God love us.

Ponder instances from today or the last couple of days in which by showing love, you have let God love you.

*Respond* I know that learning to love will take me a lifetime, but let me start right now. Lead me to love, O God who is love. Let me finally and gratefully open myself up to you, the Great Lover:

> Batter my heart, three person'd God . . .
> Take mee to you, imprison mee, for I,
> Except you'enthrall mee, never shall be free,
> Nor ever chast, except you ravish mee.

(John Donne)

## Acknowledgments *(continued)*

The scriptural excerpts on pages 8–9, 13–14, and 14; the first two excerpts on page 19; the excerpt on page 21; the two excerpts on page 21; and those on pages 24–25, the second excerpt on 26, 42, 51, 59, 73 are from the New Revised Standard Version of the Bible. Copyright © 1989 by the Division of Christian Education of the National Council of the Churches of Christ in the United States of America.

The scriptural quotation on page 16, the second quotation on page 32, the two excerpts on page 37, and the quotation on page 57 are from the New Jerusalem Bible. Copyright © 1985 by Darton, Longman and Todd, London; and Doubleday, a division of Bantam Doubleday Dell Publishing Group, New York. Reprinted by permission of the publishers.

The third scriptural quotation on page 19, the quotation that spans pages 25–26, the quotation on page 30, the first quotation on page 32, the psalm on page 33, and the scriptural quotation on page 91 are freely adapted and are not to be interpreted or used as official translations of the Scriptures.

The psalm quoted on page 67 is from *Psalms Anew: In Inclusive Language,* compiled by Nancy Schreck and Maureen Leach (Winona, MN: Saint Mary's Press, 1986), page 64. Copyright © 1986 by Saint Mary's Press. All rights reserved.

The excerpts in the dedication and on page 60 by William Carlos Williams are from "The Ivy Crown" in *The Collected Poems of William Carlos Williams: 1939–1962, Volume II,* edited by Christopher MacGowan (New York: New Directions, 1946), pages 287–290. Copyright © 1944, 1948 by William Carlos Williams. Reprinted by permission of New Directions, New York, and Carcanet Press Limited, England.

The excerpt on page 8 by Bayazid is from *The Song of the Bird,* by Anthony de Mello (New York: Image Books, 1982), page 153. Copyright © 1982 by Anthony de Mello. Used by permission of Doubleday, a division of Bantam Doubleday Dell Publishing Group. British Commonwealth rights applied for.

The excerpt on page 9 by Vincent de Paul is from *La Vie du Venerable Serviteur de Dieu Vincent de Paul,* by Louis Abelly (Paris: Florentin Lambert, 1664), pages 177–178.

The excerpt on page 10 by Teresa of Ávila is from *The Book of Her Life,* in *The Collected Works of St. Teresa of Ávila,* translated by Kieran Kavanaugh and Otilio Rodriguez (Washington, DC: ICS Publications, 1976), page 137.

The excerpt on page 13 by Robert Hutchins is from "Make it a Habit," in *Commonweal,* 21 April 1995, pages 14–15.

The excerpts on pages 17 and 20 by Gerald May are from *The Awakened Heart,* (New York: HarperCollins Publishers, 1991), pages 110 and 26–27. Copyright © 1991 by Gerald G. May. Used by permission of the publisher.

The excerpt on page 18 by Rollo May is from *Love and Will* (London: Collins Clear-Type Press, 1972), pages 289–290. Copyright © 1969 by W. W. Morton and Company.

The excerpt on page 31 by Saint Ignatius is from *The Spiritual Exercises of St. Ignatius,* by David L. Fleming (Saint Louis: Institute of Jesuit Sources, 1989), page 141. Copyright © 1978 by the Institute of Jesuit Sources.

The excerpt on page 34 about Zusya is based on a story from the Hassidic tradition, as told by Rev. Belden C. Lane on an audiotape entitled *Storytelling: The Enchantment of Theology* (Minneapolis: Bethany House Publishers, n.d.).

The excerpt on page 36 by Julian of Norwich is from *Julian of Norwich: Showings,* translated by Edmund Colledge and James Walsh (New York: Paulist Press, 1978), pages 286–287. Copyright © 1978 by the Missionary Society of Saint Paul the Apostle in the State of New York. Used with permission of the publisher.

The excerpts on pages 38 and 50 by Thomas Merton are from *No Man Is an Island* (New York: Harcourt Brace and Company, 1955), pages xx–xxi and 12. Copyright © 1955 by the Abbey of Our Lady of Gethsemani and renewed in 1983 by the Trustees of the Merton Legacy Trust. Used with permission of Harcourt Brace and Company. British Commonwealth rights applied for.

The excerpt on page 40 by Kelly Smith is from *Open Hearts, Helping Hands,* compiled by Carl Koch and Michael Culligan (Winona, MN: Saint Mary's Press, 1993), page 69. Copyright © 1993 by St. Mary's Press. All rights reserved. Permission applied for.

The excerpt on page 44 by Aesop, "A Friend in Need Is a Friend Indeed," is from the *Fables of Aesop,* translated by S. A. Handford (London: Penguin Classics, 1954). Copyright © 1954 by S. A. Handford, as quoted in *The Norton Book of Friendship,* edited by Eudora Welty and Ronald A. Sharpe, page 531.

The excerpt on page 45 by Walter Winchell is cited in *Among Friends: Who We Like, Why We Like Them, and What We Do with Them,* by Letty Cottin Pogrebin (New York: McGraw-Hill Book Company, 1987), page 37. Copyright © 1987 by Letty Cottin Pogrebin.

The excerpt on page 46 by Simone Weil is from *Waiting for God,* translated by Emma Craufurd (New York: Capricorn Books, 1959), pages 204–205. Copyright © 1951 by G. P. Putnam's Sons, renewed © 1979 by G. P. Putnam's Sons. Used with permission.

The excerpt on page 52 by Rita Mae Brown is from *Ms. Magazine,* September, 1985, cited in *Among Friends: Who We Like, Why We Like Them, and What We Do with Them,* by Letty Cottin Pogrebin (New York: McGraw-Hill Book Company, 1987), page 338. Copyright © 1987 by Letty Cottin Pogrebin. Permission applied for.

The poems on pages 53 and 56 by Mary Paquette and Janet Miles are from *Images of Women in Transition,* compiled by Janice Grana (Winona, MN: Saint Mary's Press, 1991), pages 65 and 58. Copyright © 1976 by the Upper Room, Nashville, Tennessee.

The poem on page 54 by Paul Engle, "Light," is from *Embrace: Selected Love Poems* (New York: Random House, 1969), page 28. Copyright © 1969 by Paul Engle. Used by permission of Random House.

The excerpts on pages 58–59 and 84 by Richard Selzer and Wayne Rice are reprinted from *Hot Illustrations for Youth Talks,* by Wayne Rice (El Cajon, CA: Youth Specialties, 1994), pages 93–94 and 131–132. Copyright © 1994 by Youth Specialties, 1224 Greenfield Drive, El Cajon, CA 92021. Used with permission.

The excerpts on pages 62, 78–79, and 82 by Theresa Johnson, Karen DeFilippis, and Elizabeth Alexander are from *Womenpsalms,* compiled by Julia Ahlers, Rosemary Broughton, and Carl Koch (Winona, MN: Saint Mary's Press, 1992), pages 126, 98–99, 28 respectively. Copyright © 1992 by Saint Mary's Press. All rights reserved.

The excerpt on page 64 by Willa Cather is from *Obscure Destinies* (New York: Alfred A. Knopf, 1958). Copyright © 1930 and 1932 by Willa Cather, renewed 1958 and 1960 by the Executors of the Estate of Willa Cather. Reprinted by permission of Alfred A. Knopf.

The excerpt on page 66 by Dorothy Day is from "The Scandal of the Works of Mercy" from *Commonweal,* 4 November 1949. Used by permission of *Commonweal.*

The excerpt on page 68 by an anonymous author is cited in *The Sower's Seeds,* by Brian Cavanaugh (Mahwah, NJ: Paulist Press, 1990), pages 30–31. Copyright © 1990 by Brian Cavanaugh. Used by permission of the publisher.

The excerpts on pages 70 and 74 by Anthony de Mello are from *Taking Flight: A Book of Story Meditations* (New York: Doubleday, 1988), pages 162 and 124. Copyright © 1988 by the Gujarat Sahitya Prakash. Used with permission of Doubleday, a division of Bantam Dell Publishing Group. British Commonwealth rights applied for.

The excerpt on page 72 by Vincent de Paul is from *Saint Vincent de Paul: Correspondence, Entretiens, Documents,* by Pierre Coste, translated by Thomas McKenna, and cited in *Praying with Vincent de Paul,* by Thomas McKenna (Winona, MN: Saint Mary's Press, 1992), pages 60 and 64. Copyright © 1992 by Saint Mary's Press.

The excerpt on page 76 by Dorothy Day is from "A Room for Christ," in *The Catholic Worker,* December 1945, cited in *Praying with Dorothy Day,* by James Allaire and Rosemary Broughton (Winona, MN: Saint Mary's Press, 1995), pages 46–47. Copyright © 1995 by Saint Mary's Press.

The poem on page 80 by John Ciardi, "Romping," is from *I Marry You: A Sheaf of Love Poems* (New Brunswick, NJ: Rutgers University Press, 1958), page 27. Copyright © 1958 by Rutgers, The State University. Used with permission of the Ciardi family.

The poem on page 86 by Jean Spencer is from *Images of Women in Transition,* compiled by Janice Grana (Winona, MN: Saint Mary's Press, 1991), page 61. Copyright © 1976 by the Upper Room, Nashville, Tennessee. Used with permission of the author.

The excerpt on page 88 by Thérèse of Lisieux is from the *Autobiography of St. Thérèse of Lisieux,* translated by Ronald Knox (New York: P. J. Kenedy and Sons, 1958), pages 266 and 307–309. Copyright © 1958; copyright © renewed 1996 Official Catholic Directory by P. J. Kenedy and Sons in association with R. R. Bowker; a Reed Reference Publishing Company, New Providence, NJ. Reprinted with permission.

The excerpt on pages 90–91 by Laura Thomas is from *Open Hearts, Helping Hands,* compiled by Carl Koch and Michael Culligan (Winona, MN: Saint Mary's Press, 1993), pages 15–16. Copyright © 1993 by St. Mary's Press. All rights reserved. Used with permission of the author.

The poem on page 91 and on the back cover by John Donne, "Holy Sonnet 14," is from *The Complete Poetry and Selected Prose of John Donne,* edited by Charles M. Coffin (New York: Random House, 1952), page 252.

Titles in the Daily Prayers for Virtue series

*Love* by Carl Koch

*Faith* by Wayne Simsic — Forthcoming

*Humility* by Robert F. Morneau — Forthcoming

Order from your local bookstore or from
Saint Mary's Press
702 Terrace Heights
Winona, MN 55987-1320
USA
1-800-533-8095

In the garden of the soul, virtues need tending. In prayer, we can open our heart, mind, and will to God's grace. We embrace and open ourselves to this grace by pondering and dialoging with God about what we believe, how we hope, the ways we love, and our desire to grow in moral virtue. When we ponder the Scriptures and examine our beliefs, we nourish faith. When we meditate on the goodness of God's creation, on friendships, and on all of God's gifts to us, we nourish hope. When we pray for loved ones, consider how we love, empathize with those needing love, and celebrate the love given to us, we nourish love.